WHITENESS OF BONE

GLORIA MINDOCK

Gloria Mindock 3/6/19

Alone, on the world's sharp edge
immobile now, cast in plaster.
He's not a man,
he's a wet, black void
in which nothing is visible

—Rafael Alberti

*For Elsa —
Congratulations!
Wishing you all the best.
Hope you like this.
All best,
Glo*

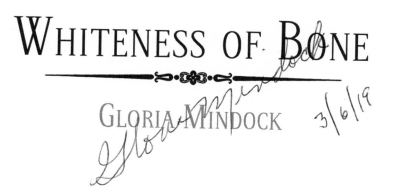

GLASS LYRE PRESS

Cover art: Tracy McQueen
Design & layout: Steven Asmussen
Copyediting: Linda E. Kim
Author photo: Mary Bonina

Glass Lyre Press, LLC
P.O. Box 2693
Glenview, IL 60026

www.GlassLyrePress.com

CONTENTS

I — In a Dark World

II — Bird

III — Rain

For Dzvinia Orlowsky

For the brave men and women I corresponded with from El Salvador, Rwanda, Darfur, and the Congo. Thanks for sharing your pain, grief, courage, strength, and love with me. I learned so much from you about the human spirit. This book is for you and for anyone who has suffered from oppression and genocide.

For the millions who have lost their lives in so many countries. We carry on with hope for peace.

We will remember you.

1   IN A DARK WORLD

IN A DARK WORLD
—for N.

You told me I was a light in
a dark world.
Hanging onto these words,
I continue.
Everyday, there is slaughter, murder,
horrific things, done to a body...
things that make me sick.

Day after day, death happens...
despite the sun coming out to
show the blue of the sky.
Beauty and ugliness in battle—
Light and dark in battle—
Each day, a tug of war and each day,
each side wins somewhere in the world.

You told me I was light in a dark world.
Why did you do this?
Do you know something I don't?
Am I an angel alone weeping
with words coming out of my mouth
that no one listens to?

NOTHING

Standing in line, I think nothing of it—
deciding what to devour for lunch.
A decision finally reveals itself to me.

Like a stargazer, I stare at the menu
against the wall.
How lucky I am when others are not.
Their shadows speak making it difficult for me to eat...
these murmuring forces cry in my head.
I answer back, everyday.

Collapsing quietly, sadly...
it is politics why you starve.
It is the big men with a circle of violence
around them splattering the people, murder on
the world's hands.

Picking up the food with my hands, I feel
its texture, a holiness as I put it into my mouth.
As it dissolves into my body nourishing me, I am
exposed for my fears.

The only dreams I have today is for no war...
where people can eat...
I must confess to you, this, so that
you will join me on this road and like a magician,
produce bread.

DROWNING

My thoughts, drowning…
until I can't remember them.
Dead in a darkness, I can't retrieve.

So many times this happens.
I stand silent, overwhelmed, frustrated.
Falling and there is no stopping it.

While my body betrays me with a heavy anchor,
the angel waits… playing a harmonica. Weird.
I thought I would hear a harpsichord or trumpet.

As my time comes closer to the end, with my
head in a book, I dream to start over again.
The sky, gray and commanding, wants me
to look at it. Then it changes to blue then green.
A force of nature with a sense of humor.

Floating towards the clouds, I'll take your hand, dear angel.
With one touch the mystery will not be important.
Transformed, right then, I will remember everything.

ASCENSION

They all were led to an embankment,
pushed over.
Shot in the head or hacked.
Piles of bodies, a crime.
The courage of those who died made
their bodies beautiful.
Ascension into the air where God touched their soul.
Evil is evil so mourning is essential.

Two lion cubs played nearby.
So cute and young…
They understood what life was but
when older like man, their innocence
is awakened by the tongue.

EYE (MISTRANSLATION FROM A ROMANIAN POEM)

If you can see the pupil in my eye, know it is an instrument
of sight, pinning its gaze on you.

I did not carry an umbrella on this rainy day,
but I will tell you one thing, you are a insensitive bastard.
Apparently, no one told you.
Well, I am the plant in the system to let you know.
Your rage has been defeated.
The volume in your mind knocked out in an instant.

Let me make this clear.

Your soul is a never-ending circle bruising itself
to black and blue.
The assault on yourself is something to see.
At the brink of war, the children can finally laugh
because they marched in on the guerillas and cried.
As the guerillas felt their tears, they dissolved.

The children went on to live with the spirit of God,
they loved singing homage to the tear.
The verse they sing of despair has been replaced.
There is no salt in their arteries.
No vinegar dumped on the ground.
No mass graves…
only a total suspense of a life now ready to live.

A New Place

My eyelids blink with an eternal flow,
heart palpitates.
As I look at the moon, so round, white—
I am seeing the meaning of our world...

Life beyond the everlasting, words creating reflections
on the window and the dimensions of each
letter says language, says the unknown, putting me
in a cage.

If I close my eyes, I am blind, need a guide.
Opening them, I gaze at everything—the planet
on display—a museum, every house, object,
all artwork for my view.
Gardens of brilliant colors intersect with me...
A lightness returning daily...

I want to capture it and take it with me
when I die.
But what if Heaven is better?
An untouched world, illuminating my soul.

ANCHOR

I was born in China
with purple feet on a
heart of voices
fluttering sounds at the saddest things

Anchor me in the China Sea
or by the Great Wall for people
to walk on
Stamp me out like an object

I wore a beautiful dress of silk and
danced alone
A scarf around my neck
A photo of me etched in stone
The inscription said: She collected tears
and friction, died in a plastic box with
hands tied, a cadaver of the bereaved

Don't worship me with tenderness but
like a wounded light

gleaming

SACRIFICIAL SUICIDE

Hands are holding hearts into the air.
Red, with blood dripping down
to the ground.

This is not a civilized thing to do.
Soon, the hearts will all turn
crusty and disintegrate.

The place you lived in—no longer...
All of you decided to do this yourself—
better than having the soldiers brutally
mutilate each organ.

For a brief moment, you wonder if
your sacrifice was worth it.
Was this judgment the right thing to do?

Don't worry, you left footprints on the soil.
Stones were set on your graves
to form shapes.
Something to make you smile as you
go on to a new path, a new canvass.

Think on Death

Sitting under the willow tree,
I hold an urn covered in oval crystal,
gold, enamels of black, pale blue, and white.
It is extraordinary to hold such a thing.
It is a beauty, shining... but the real brilliance, you.
As I open it, I let the ashes spill onto the
ground and keep some for myself.
Our close bond will be documented in my papers and
when I die, eventually this life will get to know us.

TONGUE

I am dissolving into the earth
so *they* don't see me.
Into a different space so
they don't kill me.

The torture would last awhile...
Questions, words, sounds of pain,
flesh creating a dark shadow...

I'm afraid but my tongue can't show it.
Silence is the best thing I can swallow,
allowing death to die of being emaciated—
its hunger can lead it to stones, miles away
from where any humans are.

My lips hurt and they're on fire.
I look at them and pretend my
body is a vase, full of flowers—
transforming into spring blossoms.

Somewhere

In the photograph, warships
Racing to go SOMEWHERE
Sailors fire missiles SOMEWHERE
Bodies pile up SOMEWHERE
Weeping SOMEWHERE
Anger SOMEWHERE
Injured SOMEWHERE
Blood SOMEWHERE
Seeping into the earth SOMEWHERE
Too late SOMEWHERE
The sky is cloudy SOMEWHERE
Skin and bones SOMEWHERE
Hiding SOMEWHERE
Smoldering SOMEWHERE
Prayers SOMEWHERE
Last breath SOMEWHERE
The end SOMEWHERE
Black crows SOMEWHERE
Makeshift graveyard SOMEWHERE
Whispering world SOMEWHERE

SOMEWHERE, SOMEWHERE, SOMEWHERE
the fallen talk, but we don't listen

2   BIRD

BIRD

I swallow words because my teeth are hollow.
There is no apprehension in my breath.
It would be a mistake and the enemy would know
to slash me. I have to re-stage my life, each day
pretending with different portraits daily.
If indecisive, my flesh will burn.
I must be safe and wait for peace
to wrap its white wings around me,
holding me like God does when communion is taken.
How can my tongue be still, perfection is needed to rip
the soil away from my grave.

OUT

We all decay into a nothingness, into
the abyss...forever.
No meaning to a life lived.
It is over.

Memory lasts only for a little while,
then disappears...
creation annihilated.
We wait for our perfect bodies to
die in torture and suffering.

How long will a wreath lay on our graves?
Only once.

Leave a rope around the gravestones
so the dead can climb out.

DANTE

I'm related to Dante. When I mention this, the
response is, "that is why you write about death."
I take this as a compliment and laugh. Yes, this is why.

Words float in space immortal—
float into the brains of the public.
Dante, Hell is here and people are killing
each other.

Living is not what I expected it to be.
It was an interesting life, catastrophe after catastrophe.
Time moves, collecting death for its museums—
graveyards of souls.

When I reach to grab on, there is nothing to
grab onto, no assistance from anything.
Ashes blew overhead.
I turned out the light in my house
out of respect.

Hell is a silhouette Dante—
waiting to strike with long fingers,
huge fingernails.
Killing, leaving blood stains which disappear
leaving us all in exile from earth.

LIGHTNESS

I am terrified of the night, darkness,
lit up only by the moon, the stars.
Each dot, a graveyard owned by the angels.
It is no accident that I look up and see them.

If I could, I would fly up,
touch each star, connecting them to each other.
A brightness would happen like no other,
no dead on earth rotting, disintegrating or being
eaten by bugs.
A lightness, letting all souls pass a barrier
kissing the universe hello.

ADVENTURE

The rain hits the earth
with such force, soaking the ground,
cleaning it up for its next adventure.

When the sun appears, everything dries,
is normal again—
over and over this happens.

Love is the same way. Someone is always
falling in love.
Don't be deceived by such happiness...
the world is a catastrophe and you must
fight against it.
Survival is better with perfect teeth.

There is always a gun being pointed at someone.
There is always a gun being fired.
There are always explosions, knifings, a machete swinging.
No end to these images.
So many coffins lined up, makes me shiver.

Love can remake you, give you a pain.
Love is an ode you owe yourself—
walk down the street and the road will follow.

Misery is something you slip on once in awhile.
A nightmare, you can wake up from,
with eyes open, no tears shed, an eternity...

Breathe a sigh of relief. You aren't alone.
Your flesh was only asleep.

DON'T

Don't tell me my writing is too graphic
for you as you sit in your nice apartment,
enjoying the day, sleeping peacefully at night.

You can do this, they can't.

Laying on the ground in the dirt, afraid to sleep,
the villagers wait for death, machine guns, knives,
to take them out.
Women are raped, clothes taken,
left to die in their nakedness.

Don't ask why I write about the horrors in the world.
It could be you. But it is not.
Imagine what it would be like to have your
son killed or your daughter taken,
or see your children with no legs?

Tell me, where do these people go for help.
You know where to go.

Don't ask me to stop talking of the atrocities.
Maybe someday, you will know...
maybe someday, you won't have your comfortable place.

No wishes for you. All the stars have fallen.
Pick one up by the side of the road and get busy.

MELODY

For years, no one could rejoice.
Talking was in whispers.
No one could laugh.

The people, in the village, were dying.
Walking like zombies, existing only...
One by one, they all died a horrifying death.
Maggots crawling into their mouths—
a feast.

What will you tell your children about this world?
about the cruel dictators, the sound of
guns blasting?
What will you tell them about knives slitting throats?

The children will cry you know.

What will you tell your children about flowers not
blooming?
What will you tell them about too many coffins and not
enough soil?

Will you take time to wipe their tears and innocence away,
teach them not to care, keep their mouths shut, their soul, dead?
Such emptiness will hurt their stomachs and they
will double over, screaming...
Such emptiness will cause words to be silent.
Such emptiness will cause blindness. Will you teach
them to see?

Will you mull over what to tell them or not? Will you be blunt?

Most of all, will you teach them to sing beautiful melodies which
fill the earth... letting go the violence...

And if you listen closely...quietly,
you will hear them.

INVESTIGATING

I have been investigating the hearts of the mournful.
Such dreams that it seems like storytelling.
Waves and waves of conversations floating back and forth,
pecked off one at a time by sea birds.
I watch them circle and circle, bite with such energy, I can
hear violins in the background. Music of the Mediterranean.

The sand is pale. It needs some blood to wash up on
its shore. The air smells. What were suppose to be seashells,
are only bones.
The light in the sky—
only death waiting in silence for the next victim.

Sometimes, there is magic in love, but when it comes to
the heart, it is dark, and deep in the mud. Cleaning it off won't
bring any comfort. No romance, kisses,
so it is best to forget.

People don't take time to weep for hearts.
Bodies just blend in with all the others.
A doormat walked on daily.
We all know to wipe our shoes.

CALL

Pounding, beating...
Possessing the prey, like an
animal with no cares but survival.
This is what we do to each other.
Some defeat is on purpose and the power,
spills out of the soul.
Blood tries to swallow the world.

No end or beginning—
It just is...
The killing immense and prayers
will not stop it.
We just have to wait until it is our turn
when our phone number is called and we answer.

I Am Holding

The bones of a singer
The bones of a weeper
The bones of a hero
The bones of a mechanic
The bones of a murderer
The bones of a lawyer
The bones of a child
The bones of a aid worker
The bones of a Mother
The bones of a Father
The bones of a friend
The bones of a farmer
The bones of myself

We all inherit the dark, the abyss into nothingness.
Someone has to hold us.
God's hands came. We weren't held,
but were cradled and the bones of forever lived.

The bones of the world dissolved.

THOSE

There are those who cry over nothing.
Their syllables tangle, words come out
high pitched.
This human suffering is getting tired.
They won't exert themselves into
the holy, into understanding it is
not about them.
Mouths go on and on distracting any
chance of a temporal healing.
If you run into them, give them a
prescription for quiet.
Send their brains into no more narratives.
Let them fall as you look.

BLANK

I am passing out of this life
into the next.
I know it.
Don't ask me to explain
the Boulevard I keep seeing.

Standing in the center of the globe,
yes, the center, is always where I am at.
I see the world and signs with no directions—
just blank.
People mutilating each other
anyway they can…
These deaths filter through my nostrils.
My future is over but so
is everyone's.

Consoling myself constantly with savored language,
where will all this end?
How can this be?
In my mind, I yell to the
imperfect humans to stop.
I thought I heard an answer, but no.

As I stand here, call me the master
of fear, carrying it all in my heart.
Each beat goes faster and faster, then slower and slowest.
Back and forth like a ping pong ball.

Now, here it is. Years later and all the
same things happen,
a constant heaving of bursting veins.
Blood rules water, dreams have dried, souls are wailing,
pages turn brown, no prayer in the night,

sleep is a stranger, impatience is king,
bodies just lie there,
rotting by the murderers hand, the dictators hand,
the crazy hand, the uncaring hand.

The dead world is dead.

Nothing left. Nothing left.
Nothing to cling to.
A curve, a roundness
circling around the sun—
life dried out...

God, here I am. No eyelashes
to protect my eyes.   My eyelids won't close.
I see it all, feel it with outstretched hands—
wanting to touch something.
Desolation, Exile, Alone,
Bleeding, Witnessing, Dissolving...
Fed-up, I furnish my last minutes
with this.

MESS

The spirit to live remains.
We fight to stay in this world.
It is ok to dream of eternity...
the earth, our companion... the moon,
our purity staring down as we make
a mess of things.

Agony is attached to our hands,
you'd think we would know better by now.

Angels know our fate and put on plastic gloves
to avoid our blood. They cry in disgust.
Still, we are loved...the murderers loved...
salvation when there shouldn't be.

The dead souls, the innocent ones,
try to come back, live like they should have but
they never had a chance.

END

Darkness covers my eyes.
I play hide and seek with black shadows, light.
Back and forth, eyes discarding their mask,
terrifying me.

The world is at war.
Who is fighting? A riddle.
Bodies tangling, crushing, sending
missiles at one another.
Hearing the blasts at the distance,
the annihilation is close.

My hands are together as I wait, but first
I must put on a pretty dress.
People are weeping, not me.
I welcome the heat disintegrating my body.
It is time to slide down to the floor,
feel the rush around me.

Nothing remains…
just a procession of bodies angling
for their place on earth.
Even in death, there is thunder.

Being Like This, Isn't What I Wanted

I don't feel anything.
My senses, gone.
Too much killing.
Population, growing.
Hearts colder...meaner.

Being like this, isn't what I wanted.
I am a mortal with obligations.

Stop the repression! Stop the killing!
Stop the mutilation! Stop the bloodshed!

Disentangle your thoughts,
quiet your arms, and drink some tea.
Calm down. Listen to the whispers
in the wind, the rain talking,
and the crickets singing.

STATEMENTS

They said: All flesh removed is good.
She said: You're sick!
They said: We'll use a machete on you.
       Annihilation.
She said: My death will be immortality so go ahead.
They said: Die bitch! (as they hacked her body into bits)
He said: It is done.
They said: Now lets move on.

The people in the village buried their dead.

The world: We close our eyes and will not get involved.
The result: Genocide
       Genocide
       Genocide

Me: There is something horrific about this destiny.
   I sit here deciding if I should go to the make shift morgue.

How can I? My heart is already buried.
If I can't find it, how can I find you?

ANNIHILATION

Annihilation is just around the corner.
Peeking through the curtains—
Any moment, we will be gone.

When I think of this, I feel paralyzed.
Did I do enough?
Will my words spin in eternity trying
to land in someone's hand?
Read with a calmness—
a poem where a person can make
their own conclusions about me.

I cannot persuade anyone to get my meaning.
My thoughts just mourn.

Random Thoughts About a Boy

Everyone has had someone in their family die because of war. If you live in the wrong country, you would be imprisoned, beaten or killed for writing or speaking about it. All people want freedom, but the dictators want them inside of a box, to be snuffed out if they speak, the lid closed. Their country becomes a coffin. Bodies piled up that the alive walk on. Killing is killing and no one should have to live with that. It is learned. Well, learn this, no one will walk on my coffin.

MISSING

The villagers died with grace.
Bravely.
Those who survived told about the dying.
Screaming was their preparation.

Some colorful houses are still standing.
When looking at them, you can imagine
their life in horror. Maybe, I really
see them—
ghosts, filmed for my eyes.

My sympathy is in waves.
They can hear me speak. Their hearts beat
faster and they understand.
They feel my breath—
This is not un-human.

Overhead birds sing about what they saw.
It is not joyful chirping.
This evening, there is a big light shinning
from the countryside.

It is my fault, I lit a match so
the world could see, remember.
The military killed them.
Why isn't the world sorrowful?
The missing are missing.

SHRAPNEL

There is too much shrapnel under everyone's skin. Everyone has been fired at, hit, straight in the heart, hurt, devastated, never to love again. Bits of damage attaching itself to the organ making it difficult to beat.

We all are broken. It is the type of world lived in today. No matter how hard we try, we can't attach ourselves back to solace. Storms just stack upon us in volumes and the destruction is heavy.

With eyes closed, we like the dark. Pretend not to be awake. It is better this way. The debris in our souls arrived in a timely fashion and climbs a vine leading to the heavens. God said this would happen. The vine stays, the debris adds up, and the angel laughs.

Taking Turns

Every generation takes turns...
A world with war cages the soul and accompanies
it to its final resting place.

People kill and it is hard to conceal,
bandages won't heal the dead.

It is destiny, a waiting room
for the grim.
Angels sing at 7:00 AM and at 10:00 PM but
no one hears them.
Silence maintains control in
the heart. Fear greater than silence.
Murder latching on to the shoulders
of the executioners.

The innocent work behind the scenes,
stepping over the dead, turning around and holding them.
They light a candle and take
refuge in the day.
The shadow overlooks everyone
and cries because it is lost.

Soon, the world's mood will be stockpiled
into their hands. They hang on to them.
Blood trickles down on its own and runs
down their legs.

Life is soft and in full view.
Memories climb into brains, a recipe,
a nosy person, a photo...
Life is crucified as everyone watches.
War on the grill.

War on war.

Missiles explode and we all
rush to the honeymoon ignoring the light.

Consciousness is the only evidence
we have of love.
Without this, we die.
God greets us and we dive right in.

DANGEROUS

You have lived here before, walked the same streets,
felt the same things. Different air attacks your lungs.
Somebody else exhaled the air you breathe in.
You think it human but it could be animal.
Breath so fierce, you have to sit down.

Nothing changes. Everyday for eternity,
you live, breathe, die, live again,
war again, over and over, power and slaughter.
One time, you are born in the right country, next time, you're not.
Face it. It's one forever suffering in different degrees.
Eyelids heavy with fear, wanting to close...
but that won't erase the damage.

AVENGING

The city, in flames
Sky, dark and ashen
Hope, gone
Blood
Flashes
Scorched hearts, bones,
Stink
What a day for life!

The soldiers put bodies into bags
Some, nearly 17, try not to cry,
try to be brave, not letting what they
see or touch bother them

At night, thoughts turn to stone
Protecting the heart is tough—
Eyes, sunken
Skin, pale
They honor the rules
Ready to fight tomorrow

with wounds avenging their silence

In Cambodia, the Bridge
(*New York Times* photo, 2011)

The bodies wrapped in woven mattes are lined up in the corridor of the hospital. Bodies of the young, old... Panic crushed the people into broken bones, hearts, skulls underfoot thinking it would make a beautiful picture in the *New York Times*. Little did they know that they would die today. Would they have dressed differently if they knew? This didn't turn out to be 15 minutes of fame but faces in a photo captured for eternity. One little boy watched the bridge fall from a distance seeing his parents plunge to their drowning. People screamed and Panic laughed. With the suspension bridge gone, water suffocated their lungs. Their families wept and the world watched in black and white ink.

WORD

If there was a word to describe war,
what would it be?
Bullet, machine gun, knife, machete, bomb...
These things kill. Bite into your flesh, caressing
you into an image captured by a camera.

Forever, a photo looked at, you look so innocent, brave,
mounted for history so no one forgets...but they do.

When you died, what were your last thoughts?
Home, family, wife, children, life, panic, good-bye...
As you bleed into the soil, it changes, you change.
Your death seems too long, too unfair.

Soon, they'll remove you from this war torn place into
a new place. A place where the nightmare ends and the
future is over.

3   Rain

WHITENESS OF BONE

The rain washes the blood
into the earth today.
For some strange reason, the
rain is only heard. No gunshots,
no screams, no wind blowing
death around, just a silence.

Bodies, unburied, sometimes
unrecognizable, motionless.
I need to cover them.
Let them rest in peace.
Nothing was accomplished
by this slaughter.
Cruel men murder and go milling
about with a mission in their eyes.

This is horrible but not unique.
There has always been war and genocide,
so many bodies piled onto the soil.
Burial sites, if you could call it that,
are difficult to look at.
Tears fall from my defenseless sight.
I must be in a dream.

Bones pushing out of bodies, filleted into
whiteness, brutal.
The dead are on a different journey with worn-out hearts.
How much can I say or do to stop this?
No one pays attention in this world.
Suffering has been here since the beginning:
shimmering, drifting, whispering, screaming, crying,
filling the void between peace and death.

All the bones saturate the ground.
One can learn about the life and death of the
dead by holding them.
I hear you, know you, there is no vacancy
in my heart as your life closes in.
The whiteness of bone, I caress, kiss and
retrieve your memories for a better life.

War Games (El Salvador)

From a young age, boys play soldiers.
Little army plastic figures, fight one
another as the boys make sound effects.
Boom, Boom, Boom, tenemos ya, estás muerto

The war takes to the backyard and the boys
pretend to fight with each other, rolling in
the grass, playing dead.
Little did they know, a few years later, this
would be a reality. The noises they pretended
to make, would be more terrifying, and watching
buddies die, would change their lives forever.

The boys wear a real uniform and a hat that
goes with it or a helmet. The color blends in
with the earth. Camouflaging their hearts.
One must protect that.
They are guarded, ready to shoot for
what they believe in or not. Fighting for
a freedom, they never had. They could
have died, if caught playing soldiers.
At 13 years old, taught to shoot and kill,
childhood gone, no tears to cry, alone,
their soul screams, "I am sorry."

SPEAKING OUT

The birds of El Salvador speak to one another wondering
if what they witnessed is a dream.
They don't know.
Bodies aren't moving and they see a feast of food waiting for them.
Maggots, flies, bugs, all sorts feasting...the birds swiftly dive in.

Today, when a refugee told me of the slaughter, I wrote a sonnet...
a love poem for the dead. Something for their souls to take
as they part with this earth.
I feel so empty because this harsh world doesn't speak too well.

Defenseless

I am defenseless...
pounding my feet on a flat
surface and if it isn't flat,
it will be.

I am defenseless, smoking cigarettes...
one after another.
My breath struggles...
How do I inhale and whisper
at the same time?

I am defenseless against El Salvador...
with hate and love, turning away from
my country...where is my forgiveness?
How can one forget a former life?

I am defenseless against the wooden floor
I walk on ...sliding
across the floor, fast—
forgetting where my country is.

I am defenseless over thoughts,
taking them into my mouth hoping
my equilibrium will balance my voice.

I am defenseless against inertia...
My eyes gaze with such complexity
that aspirin is needed.

I am defenseless when speaking...
Words lash into the air
for a home to cling to...
but the ground is full of dead bodies.

I am defenseless when I smile...
mouth awakened by a machete...
My skin is only nicked...

I am defenseless and can't stop being
with my Salvadorans...
Our silence like the waves crash
into the earth and bounce
back into our ears

I am defenseless...
a gift of surrender sleeps
as the grave nears,
the stones we want are unmarked—

blank but infinite
I am defenseless in comfort...
The precipice closes in
as we touch the hands
of angels.

CONFETTI

The confetti falls like stars,
hitting you on the head with consistency.
Then, it attaches to your arms, making
a blanket for your bones.
Such warmth surrounds your soul
making you immobile.

Standing there, you taste the moon as
breath encircles, like outer space engulfs
the planets.
You are now spinning into exile.

With outstretched arms, the confetti
leaves you bare as you shake it off—
walking on with no remainder.
Vanquished, like your ego.

Confetti, lying there on the floor
in different colors, alone,
swept up by a broom for
another universe,
a morgue for your voice.

STRENGTH

When shadows fell on my heart,
I became fulfilled.
Now, I have felt everything
there is to feel.
Today, I am silent and cannot be salvaged.
The murders took my speech.
There is no recovery.

From the moment the slaughter happened,
I fell into the abyss.
There, I will wait for the other villagers to join me.
They will.

Finally dreaming, death carries me to a new space—
a blackness panting on my tongue…
Oh my people of El Salvador,
we will be together to nurture our strength…

They questioned us, shot us, raped us,
hacked us with machetes, their favorite…
But I am beginning to laugh again which they cannot hear.
We all got up from the ground in an instant—opened our eyes.
We picked the flowers and threw them at death.

FOR AMAYA

Alone, hiding in a ditch, listening
to gun shots, afraid to move...
Screams buried into the dirt.
Husband, children, relatives, friends, shot,
hacked.
The men, their arms are bold as they swing.
How much blood did this planet drink?
A landscape of red.
Flesh cut deep on display.
Existence disappeared but memories live.
As the years go by, the calendar marks it.
In El Mozote, there are bones for the
archaeologists to dig up.
A grave so deep...
Lives intertwined.
Shadows covering
everyone with a blanket.

MARIA

Pale eyelids, dark brown eyes—
searching for escape.
What will it be today? A machete or a
gun that dooms your face
into that final photo.

Little girl, you had no choice but to
grow up quickly.
In your nine years of life,
someone should have told you the
whole world isn't like this.

When you walked up to the mass grave,
you saw your Mama. Twisted body,
dried blood, and decaying skin.
You crawled into the stench and held her.
No tears—just a girl wanting
her Mama back.

Staying too long, you played dead as the
soldiers passed by laughing at what they did.
With fear gripping your tongue,
you didn't scream.
Your bravery, something to tell later.

When you left the grave, the image stayed in your eyes as well
as a piece of cloth from your Mama's dress.
See her smile as you cooked supper together.
Hear her laugh as you played.
Hear her tell you not to wander too far away.
All these things a Mother does.
The cloth now pressed close to you.

Another family saved you, escaping
on a long and sometimes frightening trip.
In southern Illinois, refuge was taken. And as I
listened to your story, I took your hands
as you finally cried.

FLOWERS OF BONE

She entered into a wall of flowers that
led to the graveyard.
There were no markers… just naked grass,
so green, from the bodies that made it that way.

Maria's footsteps were quiet on the ground.
Her heart felt tragic and the silence was of defeat.
She knew there was death beneath…
Flesh, bones, body parts wrapped up by the earth—
a present of suffocation, slaughter, fear, and anger.
Her country torn apart and the tanks coming.

If caught, she would be killed
for coming to this field but she didn't care.
Everyone came here to weep.
This was the only place to have company and not be alone…
A place where the dreams of the dead float above ground.
Running her hand over the grass,
the dreams attached themselves to her.
Maria living her life for them.

Flowers bloomed at the entrance and kept blooming.
The bond she had with the graveyard was enormous.
A gift from the dead for all who enter.

Maria's home is gone, so many crimes…
As she leaves the burial ground, her head bows…
Maria picks a flower and walks.

PIECES

Her head, full of stabbing pain, stress.
Maria walked against time and felt
doom in the new city.

People rushing with eyes downward. No one noticed her
or that she was lost.
On the bus, the people were speaking and she didn't understand.
Such a lonely feeling knowing she was going to make beds at a hotel.

Maria felt like she was falling into hell,
just a nobody in a sphere surrounded by objects, breaking…
sharp and cutting.

FOR MARIA

Not everything has to be despair.
There is a gentleness about those who surround you.
Wind blowing
Sky blue
Puffy clouds
Green grass
Singing birds.

It has been awhile since you felt this.
Life filling you with voice.
Life filling you with tomorrow.
You, listening for meaning.

Open the window.
There is no gunfire here or
machetes swinging.

Open your eyes and inherit
what remains.

Maria's Uncle

Maria had his guts in her hands, tried to push them back into his body thinking it would save him. She couldn't. Screaming into her palms, his intestines touched her lips. She cried such sorrow, the abyss shook.

Now Maria travels the world, speaking about the dead, telling the world it is hopeless, that no one is capable of a quiet tongue.

With outstretched hands, she handed everyone a flower, said: you must water it to live, but if not, the depths of hell will assign you a seat.

GOD'S BIRD

Because you shot so many people,
a blackbird has found you.
It sings of death, as it
lands on your left shoulder and pecks at your ear.

Deported to a country your parents fled, you feel destroyed.
Trembling with fear, not understanding the culture or language,
you do the best you can, pick up a gun, join the masses of the young.
Hate is in your veins and the thunderstorm carries you.

Do you hear the blackbird's song?
It cries but hidden underneath its feathers is light
only the innocent can see.
You see the dark slick feathers and kill it.

Night falls and the earth flutters.
A light appears out of nowhere spreading its
love for the faces of the dead.

BLOOD STAINED WITH LOVE
−for Miguel

Bullets fly...
Shells on the ground—
decorations for the dead.
One man swears before
taking his last breath.

A slaughtered child on the road
reeks of betrayal.

Whoever fired a gun will see hell.
Doesn't matter what side you are on.

Bury the bodies, think of the cruelty.
Touch the graves with a humble smile.
Your loved ones were a privilege,
blood stained with love.

TREE

I cannot look at trees anymore.
All I see is a finger, a lung, hearts, and intestines
hanging from the branches.
The soldiers tried to scare me into mercy.

There are no leaves to notice.
Even though I survived, my sight sees
my village, friends, family…
hanging—
On one finger was a ring,
my husband's, and I knew he was gone.

I stumble now in this life
petrified of trees.
Once they gave me shade, fruit
but now only sorrow, grief.

I can't walk past them now
without thinking of rain…
without thinking of black…
without thinking of an endless abyss…

DEAFNESS

All over the world,
the building blocks of death.
No questions asked.
No dreams reached. Life cut short by greed.
Bullets hit bodies and the soil
grabs the blood. Holds it but
there is no nutrition.

Grief is heard all over the world, but the
world forgot to take out its earplugs.

ESCAPE

Inside, I am screaming—
a scar is carried on my
chest...heart...
Heavy.
I cannot forget the mutilated bodies I saw.
Deaths so brutal, I cringe.

After the 12 year war, a different
country rose from the ashes and bones.
Still this house remains unfinished.
Power still slaughters the Salvadoran people.
Gangs, government...
their demands are loud and my
voice still speaks in their landscape.

In such existence, escape
is longed for. Planned down to
the crooked smuggler found. Money
in an envelope handed over with
no eye contact. Bravery, hidden in trucks.
Traveling falls into place with rosary beads
in their hands, each bead a prayer to Romero.

Living is a taste I really want for them.
Escaping, a betrayal to El Salvador but
the pavement to a new life is calling.

In America, they have a dialogue
with themselves.
Crying and mourning, loss, a way of life
until the joy of a new oxygen takes over.

Meanwhile, I speak for them. Putting my hand
again on their soil…taking the role of an angel, anointing their
foreheads with a soul of a dead one, and they
will never forget home.
Still, this house is unfinished.

TUMBLING

With anger in your heart and a body that
wants to fight, you have to let go.
You are not at war in this country.
There are moments of crickets chirping,
lightning bugs, and a beautiful moon.

Stop.
Look up at the sky.
Tonight you are safe adjusting to your new home.

The people, your audience to talk to.
Each word that comes from your mouth, innocence…
a kind of love, fragile and graceful
tumbling into infinity.

EXPECTATIONS

So many wars—
Darkness unexpected
Fireworks for my face
A road opened

As soon as sleep walks
into my eyes, I dream of
trust, happiness, love and
good intentions
Soon, it is too little for days,
night, sky

Watching people cry, what about breath?
Breathing in and out is a magnet for
my nose

The country is tattered
Bombs explode in certain areas
Occupying aloneness

What is happening?

Protection is a venture
Something valued
Tomorrow, silence will hit
the wounds

Aimlessly wandering with glasses looking,
my passport is ready
An invitation to leave preoccupies me
while standing in the doorway

A secret, a puzzle
Not understanding…
I tell you, I need extra hours

DARKNESS

Darkness falls, skin moist,
head heavy.
Living here feels like doomsday—
a sickness rotting the body.
To die for this?

He escapes, illegal now...
Eyes sore, body cold, place to
stay, dirty and grey...
Gauntness, sadness, grief.

After months, a job, in a field...
happy to find employment.
Alive and better, he smiles and the
trembling disappears.
Friends made, he can drift to sleep
dreaming of home, and someday going back
to his country.

Perhaps he will go and silence the cruelty that
made him wrestle with death.

LISTEN

The soldiers fire into the people,
grabbing women and young girls,
shoving bottles where no bottles should be.

The soldiers beat them until lips are cracked,
rape them again.
There is no boundary not broken.

The stories travel from country to country.
The world says, "There is no proof."

So many died without a burial
or casket.
So many died in pits, unaccounted for.

Can't you hear their weeping
around 2:00AM?
How can you sleep?
How can you when the world
holds such a stench, holds so many bones?

Sorrowful Air

The terrorist walks down the aisle.
How many of us can he can get
if he acts now?

The bomb goes off, blood and body
parts strewn, fragmented all over.
All for the love of the glow, of the
smoke, blowing up into the air.
The dead seem to hold on to the
earth, the wreckage looks
like a nest for some wild beast.

Only those left, the witnesses, the living, feel the pain,
cry, covering hearts with hands, bow heads.
Their sounds are loud.
Many spirits descend on this sun-streaked day
that turned cloudy.
Hope was abandoned in the bloody sky as
grief touched our lungs.

KARACHI, PAKISTAN

3 children, all under 5
sit on a hospital bed, covered
in blood.
A bomb exploded and these children,
survived.

From this photo, in the New York Times, I could
see fear in their eyes. The middle child, had the most
blood covering his body.
I wonder, what was he thinking?

There is no end to the blood flow and
there never will be.
Bombs will continue and bodies will pile up.
Many, won't know what hit them, but these
children will never be the same.
These children, won't dream because they won't sleep.
Forever, in their eyes will be the site of the
dying, the smoke, the building shattering
around them and as the mess is cleaned up
and no evidence remains, who will clean
the children, blood forever exposed on them.
I wonder, what are they thinking?

Rwanda Interview

How do I shake hands with the mass murderers
to get an interview?
Knowing that those hands swung a machete.
Slaughter in motion.
The Hutu annihilating the Tutsi.
A well planned elimination.

Do I really want to hear their explanation?
What fueled them? Why this deed?
What morals are left as the blood flies?
To what point does the torture stop?

*"Kill them all. That is how it is."
*"Get them, hack them down with a machete, hit them with a club,
pull them apart, dump them and continue on."

How do I interview this?

* "Worse than War" by Daniel Jonah Goldhagen

RWANDA VISIT

My veins are closing
stopping blood
awakening the bone
White sticks shrieking and the
marrow turns into clouds,
floating…
loved by the sky and the sun
gives my dead body hope.

When the machetes swung,
hearts bled all over the country
and the earth sucked the blood up
through a straw
leaving dryness, a cracked surface
where the stars slid down into for fun.
Their brightness turned violet and death
got lost…

Abandoned and lost,
I saw night.

THE KILLING OF THE MAYANS, GUATEMALA

"Use anything to smash a kid with."
Lift up a rock, grab a tree branch,
anything large, destructive.
Shoot the bigger kids, the ones you
have trouble handling.
Leave your mark.

The Mayan elimination is one you don't hear much about.
Excessive cruelty eliminating a people.
As I walk in this country, I know I am walking on the
graves of the children.
Their bodies are the soil I lift with my fingers.
My heart heavy, aching... as I see photos of the
bodies in my mind.
Oh children, the world turned away and didn't help you.
Your death now penetrates the thoughts of the ignorant
in the world. Guilt. I have made them aware,
as I sit here on your sacred ground and shed tears.

Quote is from "Worse than War" by Daniel Jonah Goldhagen.
Some of the first stanza has been paraphrased from the book.

KILL

The Janjaweed attacked the village,
raped the women out in the open, and
took their clothes. A wave of horror
surrounds them, hopelessness.

So many throats slit today. What was
once comfortable, isn't.
What was once beautiful, isn't.
There is no fresh air, just the sound
of explosions and smoke filling the air.
Screaming is heard over all other sounds.

The world is witness. They do nothing.
2.5 million displaced, telling stories but
no one hears.
*They wait for the "white people" to help.
Their tears fall as all hope is buried.

*From the film, "Darfur Now."

ORCHESTRA

I don't think I understand who I am—
Bohemian girl, who never sleeps...
Can I speak to you about my poetry?
Listen, you will hear new words
coming from my voice.

Such restless power taps at your window
on a quiet evening begging to be let in.
Curious, you sit down and read my dreams of regret.
Can you hear me screaming as this world
kills one another?

El Salvador, Rwanda, and Bosnia, I am your messenger.
A girl who talks every night to the stars.
One by one, they listen and are confused,
they die out without solution.
Four billion years and man is still igniting the shadows.

ACKNOWLEDGMENTS

Bagel With the Bards Anthology: "Orchestra," "Maria," "Dangerous"

City Lit Rag: "Avenging," "End," and "Somewhere"

Daniel Y. Harris & Friends: "Metamorphosis," "Anchor"

Hildagards Daughters: Six poets, women of a visionary voice (Belgium):
    "Lightness," "Missing," "Dante," "Confetti," "Karachi,
    Pakistan," "In Cambodia," "Word," "Defenseless," and "War
    Games"

Ibbetson Street: "Sorrowful Air"

Levure Littéraire: "Whiteness of Bone," "Annihilation," "Kill,"
    "Blank," "Maria," "Dangerous," "Taking Turns," and "Word"

Lost in Thought: "Flowers of Bone"

Mass Poetry (poem of the moment): "War Games"

Mediterranean Poetry: "Investigating"

Muddy River Poetry Review: "Adventure," "Don't" and "Melody"

Oddball: "In a Dark World"

Poetrymagazine.com: "Ascension," "Nothing"

Soul Lit: "A New Place"

Tell-Tale Inklings: "Call"

We Are You Project: "Pieces," "For Maria," and "Tumbling"

Wilderness Literary Review: "Orchestra," "Speaking Out"

"Eye" was published in the chapbook *Pleasure Trout*
    (Muddy River Books, 2013)

I would like to thank my publisher Ami Kaye for believing in my poems
and for publishing this book. You made a dream come true! Thanks
to everyone at Glass Lyre Press, especially Steve Asmussen and Tracy
McQueen for the wonderful cover. You captured exactly what I wanted!

Thank you to Catherine Sasanov, Pui Ying Wong, Tim Suermondt, Susan Tepper, Flavia Cosma, Jack Scully, Doug Holder, Dzvina Orlowsky, Mary Bonina, Harris Gardner, and the Bagel Bards for the support of my writing and the years of friendship.

Thanks to my Mom and Dad, Kellis, Richard, and Alexander Dryer, and William J. Kelle who support me in everything I do. I have the best family and could not do this without you!

A huge thank you to Janie Gregorich, Carol Schmidt, Sandy Shipp and Shirley Prescott for keeping me grounded and for the years of friendship. Illinois always remains with me.

About the Author

Gloria Mindock is the founding editor of Červená Barva Press and one of the U.S. editors for *Levure Littéraire* (France). She is the author of *La Porţile Raiului* (Ars Longa Press, 2010, Romania), translated into Romanian by Flavia Cosma, *Nothing Divine Here* (U Šoku Štampa, 2010, Montenegro), and *Blood Soaked Dresses* (Ibbetson, 2007). Widely published in the USA and abroad, her poetry has been translated and published into the Romanian, Serbian, Spanish, Estonian, and French. In December 2014, Gloria was awarded the Ibbetson Street Press Lifetime Achievement Award. In 2016, she received the Allen Ginsberg Award from the Newton Writing and Publishing Center for community service.

Gloria works as a social worker and freelances teaching workshops. She facilitates events in her Červená Barva Press Studio, located in the Center for the Arts at the Armory in Somerville, Massachusetts.

Glass Lyre Press

exceptional works to replenish the spirit

Glass Lyre Press is an independent literary publisher interested in technically accomplished, stylistically distinct, and original work. Glass Lyre seeks diverse writers that possess a dynamic aesthetic and an ability to emotionally and intellectually engage a wide audience of readers.

Glass Lyre's vision is to connect the world through language and art. We hope to expand the scope of poetry and short fiction for the general reader through exceptionally well-written books, which evoke emotion, provide insight, and resonate with the human spirit.

Poetry Collections
Poetry Chapbooks
Select Short & Flash Fiction
Anthologies

www.GlassLyrePress.com